GREAT ILLUSTRATED CLASSICS

THE MUTINY ON BOARD HMS BOUNTY

William Bligh

adapted by
Deborah Kestel

Illustrations by
Brendan Lynch

BARONET
B·O·O·K·S

BARONET BOOKS, New York, New York

GREAT ILLUSTRATED CLASSICS

edited by
Malvina G. Vogel

Contents

CHAPTER   PAGE

1. The Call of the Sea 7

2. The *Bounty* 21

3. The Fateful Voyage Begins:
   We Reach Otaheite 31

4. We Meet the Islanders 57

5. Signs of Trouble:
   Three Men Desert 89

6. Mutiny on the Ship 111

7. Attack on the Beach 143

8. We Survive to See New Holland 173

9. We Become Skin and Bones 201

10. Home to England 229

About the Author

William Bligh was born in Plymouth, England, in 1754. His whole life was centered on the sea. At sixteen he was living the life of a seaman in the British navy, and when he was twenty-two he became a sailing-master under Captain James Cook.

During the voyage, Bligh worked closely with Cook in making charts of the South Pacific—charts which contributed to the world's knowledge of the area. It was also during this voyage that breadfruit plants were discovered on the South Sea island of Otaheite, now known as Tahiti.

After serving on a frigate, or warship, Bligh was given command of a merchant ship bound for Otaheite—this time to bring the breadfruit plant from there to the West Indies. His ship was the *Bounty*.

The *Bounty's* voyage was interrupted by a mutiny, and Bligh and a crew of eighteen men were put to sea. They faced almost certain death through an amazing voyage of over 3,000 miles in a small open boat.

The story of the *Bounty's* voyage and of Bligh's amazing experiences in his small boat were carefully recorded by Bligh himself in his journal, which was published upon his return to England in 1790.

Although many versions of the mutiny were later published—some of which showed Bligh to be a villain and a brute—Bligh's personal version caused a sensation in London, and he was acquitted by a court martial, promoted, and sent on a second expedition to Tahiti for breadfruit.

After a continuing stormy career in the British navy and later as Governor of Australia, William Bligh died in his country house outside of London in 1817.

A Dream of Becoming a Sailor

CHAPTER 1

The Call of the Sea

When I was a boy in Plymouth, England, I dreamed of becoming a sailor. Or, better, a ship's captain! Captain Bligh, Captain William Bligh. I dreamed that one day, men would know me as one of the greatest navigators to sail the seas.

I was sixteen years old when I began my life and career as a seaman. I was an intelligent boy, with sharp eyes and a quick mind, and soon knew the ways of the sea as well as any great navigator.

The year was 1771 and England was Queen

of the Seas. The British navy had established the greatest sea empire in history; our fleet dominated the white-capped ocean from North America to India.

Ship life in the British navy was not easy. The work was hard and the discipline was harsh. The crew consisted mainly of men who were hiding from the law or common riffraff kidnapped off the streets and forced into naval service by gangs hired for that purpose.

Severe treatment was sometimes the only way a captain could keep his ship sailing and his men healthy. Food was often rotten, and fruit was scarce. Fresh water and fruit were rationed early in the voyage to prevent shortages later, for these shortages led to death and outbreaks of scurvy—a disease which left a sailor weak, with gums as soft as pudding and with bleeding from his mouth and nose.

But I enjoyed this rugged life, and I learned quickly and well how to navigate by

Hard Work in the British Navy

the sun and stars and how to guide a ship safely through shoals and along rocky coasts.

I was twenty-two when Captain James Cook, the most respected and able captain of that time, chose me to be the sailing-master on his third—and last—voyage. To be chosen by Cook himself was an honor. His ship took me to the exotic South Sea Islands. Many years later, events on these shores would change my life, but at the time, I was much too busy with my new duties to spend much time daydreaming of my future.

As sailing-master, I was chief officer in command of the day-by-day navigation and sailing of Cook's ship, the *Resolution*. The *Discovery*, under Captain Charles Clerke, sailed with us. In addition to understanding the tides and winds, I had to know the *Resolution's* every line, all her rigging and sails, and the combination of all these that would guide the ship where I wanted her. It was a

A Sailing-Master

responsible position, and an exciting one.

We were searching for the Northwest Passage—a water route from the Pacific to the Atlantic, across Canada and northwestern North America.

Captain Cook and I worked long hours over logs and maps, recording our sightings and the characteristics of the currents. We were the first men to chart the size of North America, calculating the land to be over 4,000 miles from west to east!

We sailed north to the Sandwich Islands (Hawaii) for rest and repairs, for we were short of food and our ships leaked. Enroute, we sailed by an uncharted island, a high round rock, which Cook named "Bligh's Cap" after me.

We sailed into Kealakekua Bay in 1779. It was here that our brave captain, who was my friend and teacher, was killed, beaten to death by natives who thought he was a god

Cook Names the Rock "Bligh's Cap."

and would return in another body. During the violence, I was put in command of the seamen trapped on the beach. We were able to repair our masts and return to our ships between skirmishes with the natives. Captain Clerke of the *Discovery* took over command, and we continued our voyage.

We arrived in England again after more than four years at sea to find England at war with her colonies and with France, Spain, and Holland. I was appointed master of a frigate and was soon involved in a violent battle in the North Sea. Two months later I became a lieutenant and at age 27 was a commissioned officer able to hold the highest command.

But then the war ended. To support my wife and family I took command of a merchant ship that traded in the West Indies. There, Sir Joseph Banks, a renowned scientist and the naturalist on Cook's first voyage,

14

A Violent Battle in the North Sea

became interested in a project to transplant breadfruit from Tahiti in the South Seas to the West Indies. He planned to raise the crops as cheap, nourishing food for the black slaves there.

The breadfruit is so well known that for the best description of it I repeat the account which Captain Cook wrote during his first voyage:

"The breadfruit grows on a large tree. Its leaves are often a foot and a half long, dark green, and oval in shape. The fruit is about the size and shape of a child's head and grows on the boughs like apples. The natives gather it while it is green and hard. Then they bake it in an oven until the outside is burned black. The black crust is scraped off and a tender crust is left. The inside is soft, tender, and white, like a loaf of bread. Thus the natives plant their bread."

The Natives Use Breadfruit.

THE MUTINY ON BOARD H.M.S. BOUNTY

Banks knew that four of my sixteen years at sea were spent charting and exploring the Pacific waters. He suggested that I be given command of the ship that would travel to Tahiti in the South Seas and transport the breadfruit back around Cape Horn at the southern tip of South America and north to the West Indies.

The ship chosen was the *Bounty,* and the voyage I began was to be one of the longest and most dangerous trials of my life. It fills my head now. Vivid impressions rush into my mind—the warm, sweet breezes that stirred the palms over my head, native men and women whose skin was tanned bronze by the sun, the beauty of my ship under full sail, my men each at his station ... then the sudden turning of these same men against me. It is hard to believe that such an upheaval, such a mutiny, ever took place, for the voyage began like any other....

The *Bounty*

Bligh Is Appointed Captain.

CHAPTER 2

The Bounty

I was appointed to command the *Bounty* by the Lord High Admiral of Great Britain on the 16th of August, 1787. The *Bounty* was a small ship—ninety feet long on deck. Although she had been built only three years earlier, she was now remodeled and refitted for this voyage.

Because much of the space below deck was needed to hold the breadfruit plants, our quarters were smaller than usual. I knew this was necessary, and I hoped it wouldn't lead to short tempers when the *Bounty* was

at sea. We would be away a long time in a
remote part of the world, and the men had
to work together, or the whole ship might go
down.

In the cockpit—a sunken space near the
stern—were the cabins of the gunner, the
surgeon, the botanist, and the clerk, with a
steward room and storerooms. The great
cabin—the large central cabin below
decks—was rigged as a temporary hothouse.
It had two large skylights and, on each side,
three small covered hatchways for air. It was
fitted with a false floor cut full of holes to
hold the garden pots. The deck was covered
with lead, and pipes at the foremost corners
of the cabin had been installed to carry water
drained from the plants into tubs below for
future use.

I had a cramped cabin on one side of the
great cabin to sleep in and a place near the
middle of the ship to eat in. On each side of

The Great Cabin is Rigged as a Hothouse.

this apartment were the berths of the mates and the seamen. Between these berths the arms chest was placed. The master's cabin, where the key to the arms chest was kept, was opposite mine. It is necessary to understand all these locations because of events which would occur here later in the voyage.

The *Bounty* could hold about 200 tons of supplies. She had stores of food for eighteen months. In addition to the usual provisions, we had sauerkraut, dried malt, and barley and wheat in place of oatmeal. I was also given ironwork (files, saws, and axes) and trinkets to trade with the natives in the South Seas. I received a timepiece from the Board of Longitude. The Board was set up by the English government. Their job was to invent timepieces that would keep accurate time on a ship despite bad weather and the high winds that often knocked them about.

I gave specific directions that only 19 tons

Loading Stores of Food for Eighteen Months

of iron for ballast should be taken on board, instead of the usual 45 tons. Ballast is anything heavy that is carried in a ship to give it stability in the water. The weight of all our provisions would supply the rest of the ballast needed. I believe that many of the misfortunes other ships met in heavy windstorms were caused by too much dead weight in their bottoms. I would not make this mistake on the *Bounty*.

I will now describe the nature and plan of the *Bounty* expedition so that you may know every detail necessary to understand the following pages.

I was directed to put to sea in the *Bounty* at the first sign of favorable wind and weather. Once out of the English Channel, I was to proceed southwest in the Atlantic towards the tip of South America, around Cape Horn, and northwest to the Society Islands in the South Pacific. I was then to take on trees and

Ballast to Stabilize the Ship

plants, which I was to purchase from the islands' inhabitants. Then I was to proceed west towards the tip of Africa, around the Cape of Good Hope, and northwest to the West Indies. There, I would deliver the plants, rest, repair the ship, and then make my way back to England.

Sir Joseph Banks had recommended two skillful and knowledgeable men to care for the breadfruit plants: David Nelson and his assistant, William Brown. But it was *my* duty to see the plants safely to the West Indies and the men and the ship safely sailed home again.

David Nelson and William Brown

Bligh Keeps a Daily Logbook.

CHAPTER 3

The Fateful Voyage Begins: We Reach Otaheite

Every ship's captain keeps a daily logbook. In it he enters the ship's latitude, longitude, the winds, currents, sightings, and any noteworthy occurrences during the voyage. All this information aids captains who later sail these little-known waters.

Each day may seem much like the next to one not accustomed to sailing. Actually, each moment aboard a sailing ship is so full of activity I could scarcely describe it to you in these pages. For this narrative, I have chosen certain entries from my logbook. In places, I have added descriptions and background information. Together they will tell the tale well enough.

On Sunday morning the 23rd of December, 1787, we sailed down channel from Spithead with a fresh gale of wind from the East. In the afternoon, one of the seamen, while furling, or rolling up, the mainsail, fell off the yard—the thin rod that held up the sail. I heard his cry and looked up to see him swinging by his arms. He saved himself midfall by catching hold of a heavy cable that braced the mast. I breathed a sigh of relief. I did not want to lose a man our first day out!

At night the wind increased to a strong gale with a heavy sea. It calmed on the 25th and allowed us to keep a cheerful Christmas. But the following day it blew a severe wind storm from the East. Our spare yards were broken out of their chains on deck, and several casks of beer were washed overboard.

A Seaman Almost Falls from the Yard.

Only with great difficulty and risk were we able to secure our small boats and keep them from being broken loose and washed away. Another heavy sea burst against the ship and broke holes in all the small boats. Besides this mischief, much of our bread was ruined where water came in through a hole in our stern. We suffered greatly from these losses.

January 5th, 1788. We came in sight of the island of Teneriffe, the largest of the Canary Islands, off Northwest Africa. Teneriffe was covered with a thick haze, but the cliffs on its northwestern tip resembled a horse's head, with the ears very distinct.

We anchored in the harbor, and I sent Mr. Christian, one of the officers, to request permission from the governor of the island to put in for supplies and repairs from the bad weather. This request was granted.

Fletcher Christian seemed to be a good enough officer. He had served with me twice

A Severe Gale!

before, and much of what he knew of the sea he knew from me. I had often invited him to dine with me—a rare privilege for an officer only in his twenties. However, there were times when I was forced to discipline him. He was a proud and moody boy, and I took to scolding him on deck in front of the men, to keep him in his place. But I was never too harsh.

We took on fruit, vegetables, beef, poultry, and wine at Teneriffe, and on Thursday, January 10th, we sailed. Our ship's company were all in good health and good spirits.

It was my wish to sail to Otaheite (now called Tahiti) without stopping. To make certain supplies would last, I ordered every man to be at two-thirds allowance of bread. Fishing lines and tackle were distributed amongst the crew, and some men succeeded in catching several dolphins.

When it looked like rain, we stretched

Bligh Disciplines Fletcher Christian.

awnings across the decks to catch and save the water. On January 29th, there was such a heavy fall of rain that we caught several hundred gallons of water.

But the wet weather also covered everything with mildew. The ship was dried below with small fires and sprinkled with vinegar to kill the fungus. Every dry day all hatchways were opened, and all the crewmen's wet things were washed and dried.

Tuesday, the 26th of February. We brought out new sails and made other preparations for the change in weather in higher latitudes. Our distance from the coast of Brazil was about 100 leagues, or 300 miles.

Sunday, the 2nd of March. After our religious services, I gave Mr. Fletcher Christian a written order to act as lieutenant.

The change in temperature was very apparent, and I had the men put away their light tropical clothing and dress more warmly, for

Drying the Ship with Small Fires

we were entering a colder climate.

Monday, the 10th of March. I found it necessary to punish Matthew Quintal, one of the seamen, for insolence and mutinous behavior. I ordered twenty-four lashes. This might have seemed harsh, for six blows make the whole back raw, and twelve leave a man's back in ribbons. But I demand complete and immediate obedience from my men. Such whippings are not cruel or uncommon; whipping is the accepted law-keeper of the seas. I was no more stern than any other ship's captain.

By the beginning of April we had observed whales, porpoises, turtles and pintados—large mackerel-like fish. Our other companions in this inhospitable region were birds— albatrosses and small blue petrels which flew close to the water in the wake of the ship. The petrels were caught for food by floating a line with hooks baited. By giving the line a

Twenty-four Lashes for Matthew Quintel

jerk when the bird was at the bait, it was hooked in the feet or body. Petrels were all lean and tasted fishy, so we tried an experiment on them. We kept some caged up and crammed them with ground corn. In a short time they grew fat and fine, and tasted much better.

April was a time of stormy weather and great seas; sometimes snow and hailstones fell. With all this bad weather, we were losing ground, and the decks had become leaky. The ship had to be pumped every hour.

With much concern, I realized how hopeless it was to continue trying to reach the South Sea Islands by sailing around Cape Horn. We had been in this storming ocean for thirty days. The season was too far along for us to expect more favorable winds or weather. So I considered changing course and heading for the Cape of Good Hope at the southern tip of Africa, and from there eastward around New

Hooking Petrels for Food

Holland (Australia) to reach the South Pacific.

At five o'clock in the evening of April 22nd, I decided to head for the Cape of Good Hope, to the great joy of the seamen. Our sick list had increased to eight, but in other respects the men were in good health, though very wearied.

The stormy weather continued, and I found no reason to regret my decision.

We stopped for repairs and supplies on the African coast near Cape Town for thirty-eight days in May and June, and then set sail for the Cape of Good Hope. By mid-August we were rounding the Cape.

In our passage from the Cape of Good Hope, the winds were mostly from the westward, with very boisterous weather. But one great advantage that this season of the year has is that there are no fogs. The approach of a strong southerly wind was announced by

Plotting a Course for the Cape of Good Hope

the appearance of many kinds of albatross and petrel. A shift of wind to the northward and they kept away. The thermometer also very quickly shows when a change of these winds may be expected, by varying sometimes six and seven degrees.

Off Van Diemen's Land (Tasmania), I moored the *Bounty* and went out in a boat to look for the most convenient place to find wood and water. This I found at the west end of the beach.

I had been in this same bay, Adventure Bay, with Captain Cook eleven years ago, in January, 1777. But I found no signs of the natives having lately frequented the place or of any European vessels having been there since the *Resolution* and *Discovery*. From some of the old trunks of trees which we had cut down then, new shoots had grown and were now about 26 feet high and 14 inches around.

Trees Cut Down Eleven Years Ago

In the evening, I returned on board the *Bounty*. The next morning, the 22nd of August, a party was sent on shore for wood and water under the command of Mr. Christian and the gunner. There was so much surf that the wood had to be made into rafts, in bundles to get it to the boat. We were badly in need of plank—timber cut into long, broad, thick boards—for repairs.

To get these planks, I had the men dig pits deep enough for them to stand in up to their shoulders. Tree trunks were cut and laid across these pits. One man stood in the pit and one man stood above, each holding one end of the saw. In that way the saw could be held at an angle while the log was cut end to end. And so we worked for eleven days.

At the suggestion of our botanist, David Nelson, we planted three fine young apple trees we had picked up on our stop at the Cape, plus nine vines, and a number of

Planting Trees on Van Damien's Island

orange and lemon seeds, cherry, plum, peach, and apricot stones, pumpkins, Indian corn, and apple and pear kernels. The ground was rich and loamy. We marked the trees that stood nearest our "plantation." I have great hopes that some of these plants will succeed.

Tuesday, the 2nd of September. A lack of wind prevented our sailing today from Van Diemen's Land. For the first time, we observed fires from distant parts of the island— a sure sign of natives living there.

Wednesday, the 3rd of September. This forenoon, having a pleasant breeze at NW, we weighed anchor and sailed out of Adventure Bay for Otaheite. I continue to keep the men on short rations. But some of them disregarded my good advice and my example, and ate all their fruit at once, instead of holding some back. These men now show signs of scurvy; they are weak and their teeth are loose in their head. I will not

Sailing out of Adventure Bay

excuse them from their duty. They are ill because they were foolish. Every evening since we left England, there has been fiddling and dancing on board. I punish any man who does not dance for two hours every night. I do this because I need these men to be limber and ready to haul lines at any moment.

Sunday, the 19th of September. At daylight, we discovered a cluster of small rocky islands. We had seen no birds or anything to indicate the nearness of land, except patches of rockweed—seaweed growing on rocks. Captain Cook's route in 1773 was near this spot, but he did not see the islands. I have named these rocky islands after the ship, the Bounty Isles.

Tuesday, the 25th of October. At half past seven in the morning we saw the Island Maitea, a small island 40 miles southeast of Otaheite. We continued our course to the westward, and at six in the evening we saw

Fiddling and Dancing on Board at Night

Otaheite.

On the 26th, at four o'clock in the morning, we drew near to Otaheite. The whole distance the *Bounty* had traveled from leaving England to our anchorage at Otaheite was 27,086 miles. Our average rate was 108 miles each twenty-four hours. We had been at sea for eight months. The men were very excited to be anchoring at such a beautiful shore after our cold months at sea.

As we drew near, a great number of canoes came out to greet us. The natives first asked if we were *tyos* (which means friends) and whether we came from *Pretanie* (their pronunciation of Britain).

As soon as we answered yes to both, they crowded on board in vast numbers. We could do nothing to prevent it as we were trying to bring the *Bounty* safely in to shore. In less than ten minutes, the deck was so full that I could scarcely find my own men.

Otaheite Natives Crowd on Board.

The Natives Ask About Cook and Banks.

CHAPTER 4

We Meet the Islanders

As soon as our ship was anchored, the number of our native visitors increased. Many questions were asked about Captain Cook, Joseph Banks—the naturalist who voyaged with Cook, and other of their former friends. The natives had learned from a previous ship that Cook was dead, but they did not know how he died. I gave directions to my officers and the ship's company that the attack on the beach in which Cook was killed should not be mentioned.

The 27th of October. Two messengers

arrived from Otoo, who was chief when Cook was here. Each man brought a small pig and a young breadfruit tree as a token of friendship.

I walked on shore accompanied by one of the chiefs, Poeeno. I was pleased to see that the island had benefited from our earlier visits; I saw many fruit trees thriving that had not grown there before we introduced them. Everyone I met followed me as I walked; I collected quite a crowd.

Poeeno took me to his own house where his wife and her sister were staining a piece of cloth. They spread a mat for me to sit on and served me refreshments.

After about an hour, I got up to leave. The women approached me with a piece of their finest cloth, which they draped around me Otaheite style. Dressed this way, I returned to the ship.

This afternoon, a native came on board

Bligh Is Draped in Fine Cloth.

with a picture of Captain Cook, whom they called *Toote*. It had been drawn in 1777 by Mr. Webber—Cook's artist who had been assigned to his ship to draw pictures of the expedition. The picture had been given to Otoo by Cook, with instructions to show it as a token of friendship to any English ship that came.

Early the next morning I received a message from Otoo, asking to see me. I immediately sent Mr. Christian ashore to bring him aboard.

We greeted each other by touching noses—their customary manner of saluting. I was surprised to find he was now called Tinah. He had given his name of Otoo to his eldest son, as was their custom. Every chief has perhaps a dozen or more names over thirty years time.

Tinah is a very large man, over six feet four inches in height and proportionately

Tinah and Bligh Greet by Touching Noses.

stout. He was about thirty-five years old. His wife, Iddeah, who I judge to be about twenty-four, was also much above the average size of the women at Otaheite. She has a lively and intelligent face.

They came aboard with many attendants. I presented Tinah with hatchets, files, saws, looking-glasses, red feathers, and shirts. To Iddeah, I gave necklaces and beads. They were both extremely satisfied.

Then they wanted to see the ship. As I feared, they took a fancy to almost all they saw, and got from me nearly as much as I had already given them before. One article they thought much of, indeed even expected as a present, was a pair of scissors. The men used them to keep their beards in order.

Tinah asked me to fire the ship's guns. The shot fell into the sea at a great distance. The natives showed their surprise and pleasure by loud shouts.

Bligh Gives Gifts to Tinah and Iddeah.

I had many guests at dinner. Besides Tinah, there were members of his family and several other chiefs. They enjoyed their food; indeed, they seemed to have endless appetites! Tinah was fed by one of his attendants, who sat by him for that purpose. This was a custom given only to the highest chiefs. An hour after we dined, it was the women's turn to eat, for they were not permitted to eat in the presence of men. However, Tinah sat down with Iddeah and the women and ate as if he and his stomach had completely forgotten our meal.

A closeness between the natives and our men had developed. Hardly a man in the ship is without his *tyo,* or friend. Tinah stayed with me the whole afternoon, during which he ate roast pork at four different times, besides his dinner.

The natives continually bring food to the ship to sell. Some of the hogs brought today

Tinah Is Fed by One of His Attendants.

weighed 200 pounds. We bought several for salting. I also bought a she-goat and a kid.

Tinah was very disappointed to learn we had no portrait painter on board. He had wished to have pictures of his father and family.

The next morning, Tinah took me to the place where we had fixed our tents in 1777. He invited me to put the spot to the same use. We then went across the beach and through a walk delightfully shaded with breadfruit trees until we came to his own house—a small shed.

I sent David Nelson and his assistant to look for the breadfruit plants. They reported that it appeared there were enough plants for our mission to be accomplished with ease. I gave directions to my men that the islanders were not to know the purpose of our coming. I was afraid they would raise the price of breadfruit. Perhaps that much caution was

Buying Food from the Natives

not needed, but I wanted to determine the time and manner of buying the breadfruit myself.

While Nelson was out, he saw two fine shaddock trees, much like grapefruit trees, which he had planted in 1777. They were full of fruit, but it was not ripe.

The 29th of October. At break of day Tinah and his wife came again to the ship with many attendants. I served them breakfast of roasted pork. Natives all over the island had learned of our arrival, so a great many strangers from remote parts of the island were on board today.

During the afternoon, some hooks and thimbles—the metal rings inserted in the loops of rope to prevent wear—were stolen. I ordered all the natives off the ship, except the chiefs. They were alarmed by the angry face I wore. I thought it necessary to appear gruff.

Bligh Orders the Natives off the Ship.

At sunset my visitors left, carried to shore by one of the ship's boats. It was a mark of honor, and they preferred our boat to their canoes because of it. They requested a race between our five-oared cutter and one of their double canoes with four paddles. Both sides rowed very hard and fast, and both were greatly cheered on, but our cutter reached the shore first.

As the cutter turned to come back to the ship, one of the chiefs stopped it and tied a large piece of cloth to the boat hook—a long pole with a metal hook on one end. He wanted the cloth to be carried as a trophy of the cutter's victory.

The 30th of October. Today, during a half-hour sail with Tinah to the other side of the island, where we hoped to get breadfruit plants too, Tinah overheard me mentioning my plans to visit some of the other islands in this neighborhood. He earnestly asked that

A Race Between the Cutter and a Canoe

I not leave. "Here," he said, "you shall be supplied plentifully with everything you want. All here are your friends and the friends of King George. If you go to the other islands, you will have everything stolen from you."

I thanked him for his good will, then added, "King George has sent you all the gifts I bring. So will you, Tinah, send something to King George in return?"

"Yes," he said, "I will send him anything I have." He then began to name the different articles he could send from the island, among which he spoke of breadfruit.

I had been waiting for this opportunity. "Breadfruit trees are exactly what King George would like," I told him.

He promised me that a great many would be put on board the *Bounty*. Tinah was delighted to find it so easy to please King George.

Tinah Warns Bligh About the Other Islands.

On the way back from the other side of the island, we stopped at Tinah's house. I was treated to a concert of one drum and three flutes, with singing by four men. I gave some gifts to the performers, and Tinah gave me a present of a large hog and some coconuts.

During one conversation, Tinah wanted to know everything about *Pretanie,* and how many ships and guns my country had and how big they were.

When I told him we had ships of one hundred guns, he could not believe it until I drew one on paper. He said it looked as big as the hill he called Tarrah. Tinah wanted one of these large ships to be sent to Otaheite and that I should return in it, bringing him things. He particularly wanted high-backed elbow chairs and beds—items which reflected Tinah's lazy nature.

The 31st of October. At daylight, I sent Mr. Christian with a party to erect our tents on

74

A Concert for Bligh

shore. I soon followed him with Tinah and some lesser chiefs. With their consent, I chose boundaries which the natives were not allowed to enter. However, I left Nelson and eight men with the tents. These tents would be used to store the plants. Thus I had the chiefs believing I was doing them a favor by carrying the plants to King George, rather than having to spend money buying the plants from them.

Tinah dined with me on board. He demanded the ceremony of being fed, as his attendants always did for him. Even after all the attendants were sent away and we were left by ourselves, I was obliged to lift the wine to his mouth.

November, 1788. I showed Tinah the preparations I was making to take the breadfruit plants on board. He was very pleased, but he made sure to remind me that when the next ship came, he hoped King George would send

Boundaries Around the Tent

him large axes, files, saws, cloth of all kinds, hats, chairs, bed frames, arms, ammunition, and, in short, everything he could think of mentioning.

This afternoon, part of the rudder belonging to the large cutter was stolen, unnoticed by the man stationed to keep watch. Several petty thefts have been committed by natives, mostly because of the carelessness of our own men. These accidents create alarm and tend to interrupt the good terms we are on with the chiefs. I thought it wise to punish the man on watch in the presence of the chiefs, so I ordered a dozen lashes for him. Tinah and the chiefs pleaded with me not to be so harsh, but I stuck to the punishment.

The weather has been changeable, with lightning, wind, and frequent rain showers.

This was the first day of gathering the plants. We had much pleasure in collecting them. The natives offered to help, and we ac-

Bligh Punishes a Careless Seaman.

cepted their offer since they understood perfectly the method of digging them up and pruning them.

The ship's barber had brought with him from London a painted head, such as hairdressers use to show various hair styles. It was made with a woman's regular features and was well made up. I asked him to dress it. He did so neatly, and with a cloth and stick he formed a body. It was then reported to the natives that we had an English woman on board. The quarterdeck was cleared so she might appear. The "woman" was handed up the ladder and carried to the deck.

Many of the natives thought it was living and asked if it was my wife. One old woman ran up to "her" with presents of cloth and breadfruit, and laid them at her feet.

At last they found out the deception. Tinah and all the chiefs enjoyed the joke and, after asking many questions about British women,

Presents for the "Woman"

they ordered me to bring a ship full of them when I came again.

By this time, Nelson and some of our men had completed a large garden near the tents. Our garden ground planted in October had been trodden down. What was worse, the chiefs appeared totally unconcerned at it.

However, our breadfruit plants were doing well, with a hundred already potted at the tents. The large cabin on board was also completed and ready to receive them. When our plants increased to 252, I added more men to the guard at the tents on shore. From the general conduct of the natives, it appears I actually did not need to be so cautious.

The weather improved, and Tinah invited us to a wrestling match and a *heiva* on shore. The *heiva* is a dance performed by two girls and four men, wildly throwing themselves about.

We seated ourselves in a circle and the

Nelson Works His Breadfruit Garden.

dance began. After half an hour, it ended, and Tinah, Iddeah, and I presented a long piece of cloth to the performers as payment.

After this, the wrestling match began, and the place soon became a scene of riot and confusion. There were so many wrestlers inside the ring that it was impossible to keep order. Men challenge each other by reaching their hands forward and touching fingers. They begin the wrestling by watching and waiting for an advantage. Finding one, the wrestlers seize each other by the hair, but are usually parted before either one falls.

Iddeah was the general umpire. She did her job with so much skill, she prevented any quarrels or any muttering at her decisions. Because she is so large, she was very conspicuous in the circle.

Once, at dinner, Tinah and I discussed geography. Their ideas are very simple. They believe the world to be an immense fixed plane,

The Natives' Wrestling Match

and that the sun, moon, and stars are in motion around it. They often ask if we have traveled as far as the sun and moon, for they think we are such great travelers, nothing is impossible for us.

Thursday, the 13th of November. Some of my regular dinner guests have noticed that when we drink, we always toast to His Majesty's health. By this time the natives have become so fond of wine that they frequently remind me of His Majesty's health in the middle of dinner by calling out, "King George." And then they tease me until I fill each of their glasses to the brim so they may drink to his health again.

Drinking to King George's Health

Hauling Down Yards and Masts in the Storm

CHAPTER 5

Signs of Trouble: Three Men Desert

December the 1st. The weather for some time has been very unsettled. This afternoon, the wind blew fresh from the NW. By night, such a heavy broken sea came into the bay, we had to batten down all the hatchways. Though the rain came down in torrents, everybody was on deck all night. Each man was needed as the ship rolled violently.

In the morning, the wind increased. It was impossible to put to sea for safety. We hauled down yards and top masts and trusted to our anchors. The river swelled so much with the rain that the point of land on which the tents stood became an island. To save the bread-fruit plants, the men cut a path for the river through part of the beach away from the tents.

The sea was breaking very high on the beach, so I was astonished to see Tinah and Iddeah put off in a canoe and make their way through the violent surf to the ship. They each had a paddle, which they managed with great activity and skill. On board, these kind people embraced me and explained they were worried for the ship's safety.

Towards noon, however, the sea calmed. At sunset, Iddeah went back to shore, but Tinah remained with me the whole night.

Sunday, the 7th. I received a visit from the chief Poeeno and his wife. Like Tinah and Iddeah, they were concerned for our safety. Poeena said that if any accident happened to the ships I would be welcome to live with

Tinah and Iddeah Head For the Ship.

him, and that he and his people would cut down trees and build me another ship.

From this sample of the weather and the information of the natives, I am convinced that it will not be safe to continue in this bay much longer. We must sail as soon as possible.

Monday, the 8th. Our surgeon died this afternoon. He had been ill for a long time. This unfortunate man drank a great deal. Throughout the voyage, he scarcely stirred from his cabin. When he did, it was because he was dangerously drunk. He hated exercise, so he never would take half a dozen turns upon deck at a time during the whole voyage. I ordered all the other men to exercise; I thought the surgeon should know the needs of his body better. We buried him on shore, with many of the natives attending the ceremony.

Wednesday, the 17th. After a long day of

Burying the Surgeon on Shore

walking the island, Nelson and I ate our dinner and then headed back towards the ship. I was much delighted during this walk with the number of children I saw everywhere. They are very handsome and sprightly and full of tricks. They have many games that are common with children in England: flying kites, cats cradle, swinging, dancing, jumping rope, walking upon stilts, and wrestling.

Almost every day we received presents of fish: dolphin, tuna, bonito, and a few small rock fish. The natives' fishing is done mostly at night. They light blazing torches on the reefs or in their canoes to attract the fish. Sometimes in fine weather there are so many canoes, the whole sea appears lighted. In fishing from their canoes, they use hook and line. On the reefs, they strike the fish with a spear or scoop them out with small nets. Whenever there is a show of fish, a fleet of canoes immediately goes to sea. Their hooks

The Native Children at Play

are bright and used without bait; their rods are made of bamboo.

Monday, the 5th of January, 1789. At the relief of the watch at four o'clock this morning, I discovered that three men were absent. They had taken arms and ammunition. No one on board knew what their plan was or which way they had gone. I went on shore to the chiefs and soon was told that the deserters' boat had been found and that they had taken a sailing canoe to another island five miles away.

I sent Mr. Fryer, the master, and one of the chiefs after the *Bounty's* cutter, but before they had got halfway to shore, they met five natives who were bringing the boat back to the ship. This pleased me and I rewarded them.

I was determined not to leave Otaheite without those men. I could not understand their desire to remain on the island and for-

Arms and Ammunition Are Missing.

sake their families and the lives they led in England. But more, I would not allow them to desert His Majesty's service. Tinah and the other chiefs said they would bring the men back to me.

Thursday, the 22nd. I received a message that the deserters were in a house five miles away. A little before sunset, I got into the cutter and left the ship. The night was very dark and windy as I landed at some distance from the place where they were. The deserters had evidently heard I was coming after them, for when I came near the house, they gave themselves up. I discovered that their ammunition had been spoiled by the sea during their canoe trip, so they had to give up without a fight. The natives who had kept a close watch on them left us. The deserters were severely punished when we reached the ship.

January 23rd. This afternoon I punished

The Three Deserters Give Up.

one of the seamen with nineteen lashes for striking an Indian. His action was so serious and so totally against my orders that I could not let it go unpunished.

This morning I ordered all the chests to be taken on shore, and the inside of the ship to be washed with boiling water to kill the cockroaches. It was essential that we keep the ship free of all insects because of the plants.

Tinah surprised me after dinner by seriously suggesting that he and his wife Iddeah should go to England with me. He wanted very much to see King George, who, he was sure, would be glad to see him. And, he said, he would take only two servants. I had to promise him that I would ask the King's permission to take them to England, if I came again.

Friday, the 6th of February. Something happened today that worried me greatly—not only because the ship was put in danger, but

Chests Are Taken to Shore.

because it lessened the confidence and good understanding between us and the natives. The wind had blown strong the night before. At daylight, we discovered that the cable that anchored the ship had been cut near the water's edge. Only one strand of the cable remained. After repairs were made, I gave orders that one of the midshipmen should keep watch more directly on the cable. I believe a native from another island cut it. Tinah promised to find the guilty person.

It later occurred to me that this attempt to cut the ship adrift might have been the act of some of our own men. Their wish to remain at Otaheite would have come true, without danger of whipping for desertion, if the ship had been driven ashore. At the time, though, I had no idea that their attachment to this island was so strong, that my men would choose to remain here and abandon every hope of returning to their native country.

Bligh Discovers the Cable Cut.

From the 5th to the 14th of March, the wind blew constantly, with a great deal of rain. This slowed our departure plans.

The 16th of March. For some days Tinah has been busy making two fine cloaks as a present for King George. They are made of brightly colored bird feathers. Finished today, they were hung in his house, and Tinah said a prayer that the King of England might for-ever remain his friend and not forget him.

The natives show that they are sad we will be leaving them shortly. They are unusually kind and attentive.

This afternoon we began to remove the plants to the ship. They were in excellent condition. The roots had appeared through the bottom of the pots and would have shot into the ground if we hadn't taken care to prevent it.

Tuesday, the 31st. Today, all the plants are on board. There are 774 pots, 39 tubs, and

Tinah's Present for King George

24 boxes—in all, 1,015 breadfruit plants. In addition, we collected a number of other fruit and vegetable plants from the island.

I gave some last presents to my friends. Each man's native tyo, or friend, brought him presents also. I took the hogs given by the natives to individual men and added them to the ship's stores.

Friday, the 3rd of April. I mean to sail early tomorrow morning. The ship has been crowded the whole day with natives, and we are loaded with food and supplies. This evening there is no dancing and mirth on the beach as we have had all along. Now everything is silent.

Saturday, the 4th. At half-past six, shortly after daylight, we weighed anchor. There was no wind; we towed the ship out of the harbor with our boats. Soon after, the sea breeze came and we stood off towards the sea.

During the entire time that we were

The Seamen and Natives Exchange Gifts.

anchored at Otaheite, the picture of Captain Cook had been kept on the ship. When I returned the picture to Tinah, I wrote on the back the time of the *Bounty's* arrival and departure and an account of the number of plants on board.

We bid farewell to Otaheite, where for 23 weeks we had been treated with great affection which increased the longer we stayed. The natives were friendly and endearing. All the men were welcomed into the natives' homes and had the pleasure of sharing their simple, easy, comfortable ways. I'm sure some of the men found this life enjoyable, and it might have crossed their minds to stay. I know these are the reasons for the event which later ruined the expedition—an expedition that I had every good hope for.

Bligh Signs the Picture for Tinah.

Climbing Up the Mast To Get the Cup

CHAPTER 6

Mutiny on the Ship

We sailed to the south and west, anchoring now and then at small islands. I sent men ashore for wood and water in preparation for our journey around the Cape of Good Hope. We had some difficulty finding water. I could not allow the breadfruit plants to die for lack of water, so I put the seamen on rations. I ordered that the drinking cup be placed high up on the main mast. Any man who wanted a drink had to climb to get the cup and climb to return it when he was done. A man could do this only twice a day. This plan might leave a man thirsty at times during a day, but no harm would come to him from it.

Some of the men have grown accustomed to the lazy life of the natives and are reluctant to give it up. I must remind them daily that they are aboard a sailing ship and there is no time now to sit idly dreaming. These first days at sea I have had some difficulty getting the officers to fulfill their duties. It will be a long voyage back to England; we won't see her shores for a year yet. If it takes harsh discipline to complete this expedition, I will use it.

The 27th of April. We sailed very near the track made in former voyages. We have passed the Friendly Islands.

The men had some trouble at a watering place on these "friendly" islands. Because there was no chief among them, the natives threatened the ship's watering party with attack, made off with some of their equipment,

Bligh Will Not Permit Laziness.

and continued to menace them until they left the shore.

At noon of this day, we were between the islands Tofoa and Kotoo, west of Otaheite.

The supplies we received from the Indians at Otaheite are still piled on deck; it is slow work storing them all. Crates constructed by the carpenter for pigs and fowl lay about. Although I took for the ship's supply the hogs given as presents to the men by their *tyos,* I allowed the officers to keep the coconuts they had bought. I, myself, had a store of my own. A great many of the ship's coconuts were piled on the quarterdeck, and I noticed that a few had been taken. I ordered all the officers to the deck immediately and asked each man how many coconuts he had brought aboard for his own use, and if any of them had seen a seaman helping himself to one of the ship's supply. I became more and more angry as the theft was denied again and

A Few Coconuts Have Been Taken.

again. I knew some coconuts had been stolen. The men had grown lazy and irresponsible, and I was tired of their insolent behavior.

I finally came to Mr. Christian. When I asked him how many coconuts belonged to him and what had happened to the missing ones, he answered, "I hope you don't think I am so mean that I stole yours."

I shouted, "Yes, you damned hound, I do. Someone has stolen them!"

Christian turned and went below.

Thus far, the voyage had been a success, and many events had been both pleasing and beneficial. A different scene was now to be experienced. A conspiracy had been formed which would bring all our labor to misery and distress. I had no suspicion of the coming disaster. It was an unplanned and reckless move, but each man involved was willing to risk death by hanging. It was mutiny! This foul deed, the worst crime a seaman can

Bligh Accuses Fletcher Christian.

commit, was led by Fletcher Christian. I cannot understand his hatred of me, a hatred that moved him to mutiny.

I believe his first thought was to desert. We were not far from Tofoa; a raft would have made it easily. But the night was fine, and the men chose to stay on deck rather than lie in stuffy bunks below. Therefore Mr. Christian could not desert without being discovered. So he decided to take over the *Bounty*. He must have known he would have to put me off her to keep her.

The early morning watch on Tuesday, the 28th of April, was Christian's. He moved from bunk to bunk, stirring up the men against me. The majority of those he chose were men I had found it necessary to punish severely at some time during the voyage. They were pleased at this opportunity to have their revenge on me.

Just before sunrise while I was asleep, Mr.

Christian Stirs Up the Men.

Christian, the master at arms, the gunner's mate, and one of the seamen burst into my cabin. They dragged me out of bed, tied my hands with a cord behind my back, and threatened me with instant death if I spoke or made a noise.

I called out for help as loud as I could, but the mutineers had already locked up the officers who were not involved in the mutiny with them. There were three more men at my cabin door.

Christian held a cutlass; the others had muskets or bayonets. I was hauled out on deck and forced to stand there wearing only my shirt. The men around me looked mean and ugly. I was in great pain, for they had tied my hands very tightly.

I demanded to know the reason for such violence.

"Hold your tongue, sir, or you are dead this instant!" cried Christian.

Bligh Is Taken Prisoner by the Mutineers.

THE MUTINY ON BOARD H.M.S. BOUNTY

The boatswain—the officer in charge of the deck crew, rigging, and anchors—was ordered to lower the cutter into the water immediately. He was threatened with death if he didn't do it. Was I now to be set adrift? I looked at the ship's cutter. It was so rotted, so eaten by worms after our long voyage, that it would not hold the weight of a boy safely.

The boatswain protested, "It would be murder to set men adrift in this cutter."

So the mutineers reluctantly lowered the launch instead. This was a risk on their part. They didn't want to sentence us to certain death in the cutter. But they knew that if any of us lived to tell the tale of the mutiny, the British government would hunt every corner of the earth until the mutineers were found and hanged.

I continued to argue, urging them to consider their violent deeds and to put aside

The Cutter Was Rotted.

their weapons.

Christian suddenly threw down the cutlass he had been holding and grabbed a bayonet from a seaman near him. With a strong grip on the cord that tied my hands, he spun me around to face him. Holding the bayonet to my chest, he snarled, "Silence, you hound, or you are dead!"

The villainous seamen surrounding me had their guns cocked and their bayonets fixed on me. They were like hungry animals waiting for the kill.

Certain of my men were called on to go over the side and into the launch: two midshipmen, the clerk, Nelson, the gunner, the cook, and the sailmaker. I understood that I was to be set adrift with these people.

I begged Mr. Christian to stop immediately. "I'll even betray my honor," I cried. "I give you my word, Mr. Christian, I will forget all this if you will stop immediately. I will not

"Silence, You Hound, or You Are Dead!"

record it. Think of your family! Think how they will suffer!"

For a moment I thought he might have softened, but he shook his head like an angry dog and replied, "No, Captain Bligh, you have no honor! If you had, it would not have come to this. And if you had any cares for *your* wife and family, you should have thought of them before. You should not have behaved like the villain you are."

I tried to speak again.

"Silence!" he roared in a strained voice. "Or you will have your brains blown out!"

The boatswain spoke softly, trying to calm Christian.

"'Tis too late, sir," Christian said in a quieter tone. "I have been in hell for these weeks and will bear it no longer. You know I have been treated like a dog by him all during the voyage."

I did not know what he could mean.

Christian Roars at Bligh.

Treatment on my ship was no different from treatment on any English ship. Discipline was harsh, and food was often scarce. But this was the way of life on the sea.

The boatswain and seamen who were to go in the launch were allowed to collect twine, canvas, lines, sails, an eight and twenty gallon cask of water, 150 pounds of bread, a small amount of rum and wine, and a compass. But they were forbidden, on pain of death, to touch a map, a book on astronomical observations, a sextant, or my surveys and drawings.

Once Christian forced those men he meant to get rid of into the launch, he directed a share of liquor to be served to each of his own crew.

I knew that nothing could be done now to recover my ship. There was no one to assist me, and every move I made was met with threats of death.

Loading Supplies on the Launch

The officers were released from their cabins, led up on deck, and forced over the side into the launch. I was kept apart from everyone by Christian, who held the cord that bound my hands. Guards stood around me.

Some of the seamen wanted to leave the ship with me, but were held against their wishes. They begged me to remember that they had no part in the mutiny.

The clerk managed to obtain my journals and some of the ship's papers from my cabin, even though he was guarded and watched. Without them, I would have nothing to prove what I had done—that I was dutiful and honorable. But as he reached for the timepiece and a box which held my surveys and drawings, his guard jabbed him in the ribs and growled, "Damn your eyes! You are lucky to get what you have. Leave those alone!"

Mr. Christian seemed uncertain whether or

The Clerk Tries To Get Bligh's Surveys.

not he should keep the carpenter and his mates or send them out on the launch. At length he decided to keep the mates and send the carpenter over into the launch. Then there was the question of the carpenter's tool chest.

"Damn my eyes!" cried one seaman. "Bligh will have a new vessel built in a month if he has a carpenter and tools!"

The whole of the mutinous crew was shouting and swearing. Christian thought it wise to keep the carpenter's tools. He emptied the chest on the deck and dropped only a hand saw, a small axe, a hammer, and a bag of nails back into it. Then he passed it down to the launch.

"Mr. Christian," cried one of the mutineers, "what about the compass you allowed the boatswain to take? I'll be damned if he does not find his way home with it."

But Christian did not take it back. "Come,

Christian Drops a Few Tools into the Chest.

Captain Bligh," he said. "Your officers and men are now in the boat, and you must go with them. If you attempt to resist in the least, you will instantly be put to death."

A tribe of mutinous rogues surrounded me. I was forced over the side, where they finally untied my hands.

The mutineers laughed at the helpless and hopeless situation of the launch. There were nineteen of us in her. She sat dangerously low in the water, and none of us had any room.

"Arms, Mr. Christian," I called up. "We shall need arms."

The men laughed louder and shouted down, "You know the people you will be meeting well enough. You will not need any arms."

Still, four cutlasses were thrown into the launch as an afterthought.

Ropes still held us alongside the *Bounty,* and we bore a great deal of taunting from

Cutlasses Are Thrown into the Launch.

the mutineers. After some time, these un-feeling wretches grew tired of their sport, and we were cast adrift in the open sea.

A few hours before, my situation had been flattering. I had a ship in the most perfect order, well stored with every necessity for the crew's health and a safe voyage. By my care-ful storage and rationing of food and water, I was prepared for any accident or delay. The plants had been successfully kept in the most flourishing state. On the whole, the voyage was two-thirds completed, and the remainder of it appeared promising.

Now the situation was unimaginably des-perate. We were dropped into the middle of a vast, unmapped sea. The few islands near-by were peopled with savages who were friendly *only* if they knew their visitors were strongly armed and brought gifts. We were neither. The launch was tiny and open to the sky. It was so overloaded that the water came

A Tiny Launch in a Vast, Unmapped Sea

within inches of the upper edges of its sides, and only half of the men could lie down at a time. We had enough food for only a few days. A compass was our one instrument. And, most unfortunately, the best of the able-bodied seamen had remained on board the *Bounty* with Mr. Christian.

What could be the reason for such a revolt? I can only think that the mutineers hoped for a happier life among the Otaheiteans than they could possibly enjoy in England. Perhaps they imagined they would live in the midst of plenty on one of the finest islands in the world—an island where they would never have to work.

The most any commander could have suspected was that some of the men would be tempted to desert. Desertions have happened, more or less, from most of the ships that have been at the Society Islands. But mutiny and the piracy of my ship is beyond belief! I had

Enough Food for Only a Few Days

no idea of any troubles, real or imagined, on my ship during the entire voyage.

As the launch pulled away, I heard from the deck of the *Bounty* many cries of "Huzza for Otaheite!" I had no doubt of the mutineers' destination.

When we were farther from the *Bounty*, I saw that those villains were throwing my carefully gathered breadfruit plants overboard, one by one.

The Mutineers Throw the Plants Overboard.

Rowing Toward Tofoa Island

CHAPTER 7

Attack on the Beach

There was little or no wind. We rowed pretty fast toward Tofoa Island, which lay about ten leagues, or thirty miles, from us. At Tofoa, I meant to seek a supply of breadfruit and water, and then sail for Tongataboo. There, I would risk a meeting with the King. We would need much more food and water to reach the nearest settlement in the East Indies. It was a Dutch settlement, 3,600 miles to the west.

It was calm all afternoon till about four o'clock. Then a moderate breeze came up, and we were able to sail. It was dark when we got to Tofoa. But the side of the island where I expected to land was too steep and rocky. So I served every man half a pint of grog— rum mixed with water and each took his rest as well as our unhappy situation would allow. One man was needed at the oars all night to keep the launch from drifting out of a cove we had discovered.

In the morning at dawn, we rowed along the shore in search of a landing place. We dropped the grapnel—a small anchor—near some rocks. A strong surf ran towards the shore, making it dangerous to land. But we needed to obtain some food from this island, and I wanted to save our small supply for whatever might come. So I sent the clerk and some others in search of food for us.

Towards noon, they returned with a few quarts of water, which they had found in holes. They had found no spring. Since I was

Finding Water in Holes on the Island

uncertain of our future, I issued only a morsel of bread and a glass of wine to each man for dinner. The men kept their spirits high.

Next day the wind blew so strong, we could not venture to sea. We rowed along the shore to see if anything else could be gotten. At last we discovered some coconut trees, but they were on the top of high cliffs. With great difficulty, some of the men climbed them and got about twenty coconuts. They tied the coconuts with ropes, and we hauled them through the surf to the boat. There was nothing else to do here, so we returned to the cove where we had spent the last night. I gave each man a coconut, and again we tried to rest in the boat.

At daylight, we attempted to put to sea, but the wind and weather were so bad, I was glad to return to the cove. I issued a morsel of bread and a spoonful of rum to each man, then I decided to go ashore to search for more

Hauling Coconuts Through the Surf

food.

We landed on the beach, and I went off with Nelson, the clerk, and some others. We hauled ourselves up the cliffs by long vines, made by the natives for that purpose. The vines were the only way to get onto the island beyond the beach.

We found a few deserted huts and a small cluster of breadfruit trees. We came to a deep gully that led towards a distant volcano. We were able to collect nine gallons of water from the gully. It was not as much as we needed, but it would help us. We came within miles of the foot of the volcano, which was almost constantly burning. The country near it was covered with lava. It was a most dreary scene.

We returned down the cliffs, weak and dizzy, and ate about an ounce of pork at noon.

I had told the men who remained by the boat to look for fish, or whatever they could

The Volcano Was Constantly Burning.

pick up about the rocks. But nothing edible could be found. On the whole, we thought ourselves on the most miserable spot on earth.

I was not certain if this island was inhabited or only visited by natives at certain times. It was important to know. If there were a few people here, they might give us a moderate amount of food for our journey. In that case, I would stay here and try to arrange for food, rather than risk going elsewhere where we might lose everything.

There was a cave about 150 yards inland from the beach. The only way to reach it was by the vines which I have described. The cave would secure us from surprise. I decided to stay on shore in the cave with some of the men for the night. I ordered the master to stay in the anchored launch with the others, and to keep watch in case we were attacked. We supped on one piece of fruit and a half-

Climbing Up the Vines to a Cave

cup of grog each. I arranged the watches for the night, so each man had his turn, and I saw to it that a good fire was kept up in the cave. Then I lay down to sleep.

Friday, May the 1st. At dawn, the party set out again by a different route to see what they could find. They met two men, a woman, and a child. Soon, other natives came to us, and by noon there were thirty around us. No particular chief was with them, yet they behaved honestly and traded the provisions of water and breadfruit they had brought for a few buttons and beads. Those of the party who had been out told me they saw several neat plantations. There was no longer any doubt that settled inhabitants were on the island. I decided to get what I could and to sail the first moment that the wind and weather would allow us to put to sea.

I had a puzzling problem—what to tell the natives about the loss of my ship. They had

Trading for Water and Breadfruit

too much sense to believe that the ship was to join me, for she was not in sight from the hills. I could not tell them the truth, so I said that the ship had turned over and sunk, and that only we were saved. They seemed surprised, but not sad. They asked only for nails, again and again. What few nails we had I had hidden away on the launch, for there were none to spare now.

Towards evening, I was pleased to find our stock of provisions increased, although the natives had little to spare. What they brought was not enough for our long voyage. At sunset, all the natives left us peacefully. I hoped they would come the next day with a better supply of food and water, so that we might sail without further delay.

At daybreak, everyone seemed in better spirits. Since there was no guarantee that the natives would supply us with water, I sent a party among the gullies in the mountains to

Bligh Tells the Natives His Ship Had Sunk.

search for water.

While the men were gone, the natives came to us in greater numbers. Two canoes also rounded the north side of the island. In one of them was an elderly chief

Soon after, some of our party returned, and with them came another chief. I made a present of an old shirt and a knife to each chief. I soon discovered that they knew me. They asked about Captain Cook and also Captain Clerke, who had sailed with him. They were also very anxious to know how I had lost my ship.

A young native named Nageete appeared. I had seen him before, and we had a friendly conversation which pleased me. This, however, was not to last long.

The number of natives seemed suddenly to increase, and I began to suspect a plan against us. They attempted to haul our launch ashore. I swung my cutlass over my

Presents for the Chiefs

head in a threatening manner, and they moved away. Then everything became quiet again.

My men who had been in the mountains returned with about three gallons of water. I kept buying up the little breadfruit and some spears the natives brought to us.

We had only four cutlasses with which to arm ourselves, and two were in the bottom of the launch.

There was nothing we could do until sunset. If we attempted to leave during daylight, we would certainly have to fight our way through. In the meantime, I instructed the men to try to take the supplies we had bought from the natives to the launch in a casual manner, so as not to raise suspicion. The beach was now lined with natives holding stones in their hands. We heard nothing but the knocking together of the stones. I knew very well this was the sign of a coming

Bligh's Cutlass Chases the Natives.

attack.

At noon, I served coconut and a breadfruit to each man, and also gave some to the chiefs to appear friendly. The chiefs kept asking me to sit down, but I constantly refused. Both Nelson and I knew that they were planning to take hold of me the first chance they got. We kept on our guard constantly.

After dinner, we began, little by little, to get our things into the boat. The surf was high, which made this difficult. I watched the natives carefully. More and more of them appeared. They made fires and fixed places to stay during the night. They seemed to be planning their attack. I sent orders to the master—he was to keep the launch close to the shore, and when he saw us coming down the cliffs, he should have the launch ready to put to sea.

I had my journal on shore with me and I had been writing in the cave. When the journal was

A Sign of a Coming Attack!

sent down to the launch with some breadfruit, the natives tried to snatch it away. But the gunner managed to rescue it.

When the sun was near setting, each man picked up some portions of the remaining supplies and boldly carried them down the cliffs to the launch.

On the beach, the chiefs asked, "Aren't you staying the night on the beach with us?"

"No," I said. "I never sleep out of my boat. In the morning I will return to trade with you as we agreed."

The older chief rose and said, "You will not sleep on shore? Then *Mattie!*" (which means "We will kill you!"). And he left me. Every native was knocking stones together as we walked down the beach in a silent kind of horror.

I ordered the carpenter to stay with me on the beach until the other men were in the boat. As I was getting on board, one seaman

"We Will Kill You!"

ran up the beach to cast off the stern rope. The master and others yelled after him, "Come back, man! You'll be killed!" They hauled me out of the water and into the launch.

No sooner was I in the boat than about two hundred natives attacked. The unfortunate seaman who had run up the beach was knocked down, and the stones flew like shots from a cannon. Many Indians grabbed hold of the stern rope and began hauling the boat back to shore. Stones were falling all around us. The launch was inching nearer and nearer to the shore when I was finally able to cut the rope with a knife I had in my pocket.

We then pulled ourselves back out to sea on the line of the grapnel anchor which was still imbedded in the sea floor. Every man was bruised and hurt by the shower of stones. Looking back to the beach, I saw five of the natives standing over the poor seaman they

The Men Haul Bligh into the Launch.

had killed. Two of them were still beating him about the head with stones.

We had no time to think of him now. The natives filled their canoes with stones, and twelve of them left the shore and came after us to renew the attack. We couldn't get away from them quickly enough. Our grapnel line was tangled. We were stuck, and the natives' canoes were pulling closer. Suddenly, the clawed head of the grapnel anchor broke off under the strain. We manned our oars and pulled to sea.

The natives, however, could paddle quickly and had enough canoes to surround us. We were being attacked and could only return the fire with the stones that happened to fall in the launch. In our tired, worn condition, we had no strength to aim and throw the stones. We could not outrow them because our boat was cluttered and heavy. So I began throwing clothes overboard. The natives

Bligh Throws Clothes Overboard.

slowed their canoes to pick up the clothes. It was now almost dark, and they ended the attack and rowed towards the shore, leaving us bleeding and sore.

The poor man killed by the natives was John Norton. This had been his second voyage as quartermaster with me. I was sad to lose a man with so fine a character as his.

I had been attacked once before that way, with a smaller number of seamen against a multitude of Indians. This had been after the death of Captain Cook. But even with that experience, I still had no idea that a man's arm could throw eight-pound stones with the force and accuracy that these people did. The Indians knew we had no firearms. If they had thought to attack us while we were in the cave, we would all have been killed.

I had planned to head for the island of Tongataboo, but there was no reason to expect any friendlier treatment from the natives

The Natives Pick Up the Clothes.

there. Even if our lives were not in danger from them, they would probably take the boat and everything we had, ruining all our hopes of ever returning to England.

We set our sails. I tried to think clearly of what course to take. All hands begged to be taken toward home. I told them that though we might find some food at New Holland, our nearest help was a Dutch settlement that was 1,200 leagues, or 3,600 miles, away. The men all agreed to live on an ounce of bread and half a cup of water a day.

Thus began our journey across an unknown sea in a small boat deeply laden with eighteen men. We had lost much of our food stores in the bustle and confusion of the attack. A few coconuts were in the boat, but the breadfruit was trampled to pieces.

Setting Sail for a Dutch Settlement

A Violent Storm Whips the Launch.

CHAPTER 8

We Survive to See New Holland

It was night. We divided the men into watches, got the boat in a little order, and thanked God for our miraculous escape. The men seemed to have confidence in my skills of navigation, and we were all more at ease than we had been for some time past, although our condition had not really changed.

At daybreak, the wind increased. The sun rose very fiery and red—a sure sign of a severe gale. A violent storm followed, and the sea ran very high—so high that between waves, the sail was loose and flat. And when the boat was atop a crest, the wind whipped it dangerously. Our lives were in very immediate peril. The sea curled over the stern of the boat, and we bailed out the water with all our might.

Our bread was in bags and in danger of being spoiled by the water. If this could not be prevented, we would certainly starve to death. I began to examine what clothes were in the boat and what other things could be spared. I decided that only two suits of clothing should be kept for each man The rest was thrown overboard, along with some rope and spare sails.

This lightened the boat considerably and gave us more room to bail out the water. At the first possible moment, when the seas did not come so high, we placed the bread in the carpenter's strong tool chest and stowed the tools in the bottom of the boat.

We were very wet and cold, and I served a

Bailing and Lightening the Boat

teaspoonful of rum to each man. We each also had a quarter of a breadfruit, which we could hardly swallow because it was so bad. Our strict diet was enforced; I was determined to make our provisions last eight weeks, no matter how small our daily meals became.

At noon, I directed our course farther north in hopes of sighting the islands the natives called *Feejee*. I later learned that our strong, though saturated, launch was the first European vessel to locate the Fiji Islands here.

The weather continued to be very severe. The sea ran higher, if a higher sea could be imagined. Each man was exhausted from the constant bailing we had to do to keep the boat from filling with water. We could do no better than keep above each wave as it came at us. The boat performed so well that I no longer had any fears of it being overturned.

Of all our hardships, the constant wetness was the smallest. The night grew very cold,

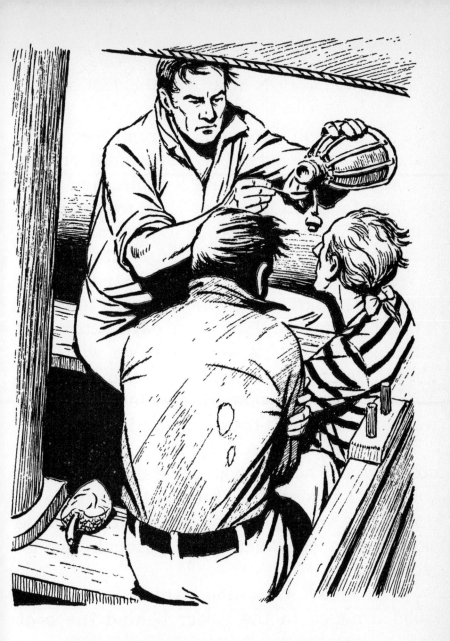

A Teaspoonful of Rum to Each Man

and at daylight, we were so numb, we could hardly move. I served a teaspoonful of rum to each man, along with a few pieces of yams that we found in the boat. Then we examined our bread. A great deal of it was rotten, but we were glad to keep it for use later.

Wednesday, the 6th of May. We passed ten islands, the largest of which I judge to be 18-24 miles around. I did not dare attempt a landing. We had no arms and we were less able to defend ourselves than we had been at Tofoa. I believed that all the larger islands were inhabited, as they appeared very fertile.

It was difficult to keep an account of the ship's run. The sea was constantly breaking over us. I recorded latitude and longitude as accurately as I possibly could, and I made sketches to show our path through the islands.

We marked a log-line, which is a bit of wood dragged in the water behind the boat

Bligh Records Latitude and Longitude.

to help us note the speed we traveled at. It was impossible for our readings to be very correct, but it helped our morale to keep records of our situation.

For dinner, I served some of the rotten bread and half a cup of water.

To our great joy we hooked a fish, but we were terribly disappointed when we lost it trying to get it into the boat.

As we were very miserable and cramped, I tried to remedy the problem by putting ourselves "at watch and watch." This means that half the men were always sitting, while the other half were lying down in the boat's bottom or up on a chest. Nothing covered us but the sky. Our limbs were dreadfully cramped; we could not stretch out for fear of upsetting the launch, and the cold and wet continued to plague us. We could not sleep for more than a few hours at night.

We discovered land again at dawn on the

Losing a Hooked Fish

7th of May. We also saw two large sailing canoes coming swiftly after us along the shore. We were afraid of their purpose, and we rowed away with some fear, fully aware of our weak and defenseless condition.

All afternoon the canoes followed us. It was now very rainy, with thunder and lightning. Only one of the canoes gained on us. It was only two miles off when it gave up the chase. It is still doubtful whether or not these canoes had any hostile plan against us. Perhaps we could have gotten food from them, but in our weakened condition, the experiment would have been risking too much.

Heavy rain came on at four o'clock, and every man did his best to catch some water. We were able to increase our supply to 34 gallons and quench our thirst for the first time since we had been at sea. We kept a fishing line towing from the stern of the boat and saw great numbers of fish, but we could

Rowing Away from the Two Canoes

never catch one.

Later in the day, the sun shone at last, and we stripped and dried our clothes. We cleaned out the boat and were busy until sunset getting everything dry and in order. I made a pair of scales with two coconut shells, and for a weight, I used some pistol-balls which one of the mutineers had accidentally let slip into the launch.

I also amused all the men with descriptions of New Guinea and New Holland. I gave them all the information I could think of, so that in case an accident should happen to me, those who survived might have some idea how to find their way to Timor. Before this, they knew nothing of the place but the name, and some of the men did not even know that.

Saturday, May the 9th. Today we ate the remainder of the rotten bread, which was edible only by people in our wretched starving condition.

Bligh Makes a Scale with Coconut Shells.

THE MUTINY ON BOARD H.M.S. BOUNTY

In the afternoon, we ran a pair of lines from the top of each mast to the boat's sides to keep them more stable. We also fitted a canvas weather cloth around the boat to raise the sides. This helped to keep the water out.

Monday, the 11th. In the morning, I served everyone a teaspoonful of rum. Our limbs were so cramped, we could scarcely move them. Our situation was now extremely dangerous. The sea frequently ran in over the stern, which kept us bailing with all our strength. At noon the sun appeared. We were as pleased as we would have been if it appeared on a winter's day in England.

In the evening it rained hard, and we experienced another dreadful night. I thought the morning would never come. It showed me a miserable set of people, full of want, without any hopes to relieve them. Some complained of great pain, and everyone was close to losing all use of their limbs. The little sleep

A Canvas Cloth To Raise the Boat's Sides

we got was not refreshing at all, for we were covered with sea and rain. There was no way to dry our clothes. I recommended that everyone strip and wring out their clothes in the salt water. The sea water was warmer than the rain. In this way we were a bit warmer, though still wet.

Friday, the 15th. At one o'clock in the morning, another group of islands and a number of sea birds were seen. The sight only increased the misery of our situation. We were very close to starving, although plenty of food was in view on the islands. But we had no means of getting it without exposing ourselves to danger. However, I do consider the cloudy and wet weather to be for our benefit, for in hot, sunny weather we would have died of thirst. The rain protected us from that dreadful end. And even our constant bailing to stay afloat was not a bad thing, for it gave us much needed exercise.

Wringing Out Clothes in Sea Water

The little rum we had was of great benefit when our nights were particularly bad. I generally served a teaspoonful or two to each man. It was always good news when I mentioned the rum bottle.

Monday, May the 18th. The rain slowed, and we stripped and wrung our clothes through the sea water as usual. Every man complained of violent pain in his bones. I was surprised that no one was dangerously ill yet. I saw many sea birds—a sign of being in the neighborhood of land.

Wednesday, May the 20th. Constant rain, always bailing. At dawn, some of my men seemed half-dead. Our appearances were horrible. Every way I looked I caught the eye of someone in pain. Our extreme hunger was now visible, as our ribs were showing. But no one suffered from thirst. Sometimes we were so covered with rain and salt-water, we could scarcely see.

Always Bailing

Everyone dreaded the night, for the misery we suffered then was overwhelming. The sea foam flew over us with great force, and we bailed, full of horror at its strength. I began to fear that one more night like this would put an end to the lives of several of our men, for they seemed unable to continue with such sufferings. Our clothes were now so threadbare, they would not keep out the wet or the cold.

As the days became clearer and the sea began to run smoother, we took in little water. I took the opportunity to check our bread supply. According to the amount given daily, we had enough left for 29 days. I hoped we would be able to reach Timor by then. But it was possible that we might have to sail to Java because of unfavorable winds or other causes. It was settled that I would begin dividing the food that was left to make it last for 43 days.

The Misery is Overwhelming.

Monday, the 25th. At noon, some sea birds came so near to us that one of them was caught by hand. It was a noddy—a bird about the size of the pigeon. I divided it in 18 portions and gave it out by a well-known method at sea called *Who shall have this?*

This was done by having the clerk turn his back to me. Then, as I pointed separately to each portion, I asked, "Who shall have this?"

Each time the clerk would name one of the men in the launch, I gave that man his portion. This method gave every man a fair chance at the best share. The bird was eaten up, bones and all, with salt water for a sauce.

In the evening several boobies flew by Boobies are birds as large as ducks, and we had the good fortune to catch one of them. The booby had received its name from seamen because it flies into the masts and yards of ships and gets itself caught. The booby we caught was killed for supper, and its blood

194

Who Shall Have This?

was given to three of the men who were the most in need of food.

Tuesday, the 26th. In the morning we caught another booby. Towards noon we passed a great many pieces of branches of trees. They didn't appear to have been in the water a very long time.

I gave each man his share of bread, and to make it taste better and to soften it, most of the men dipped it in salt water. I generally broke mine into small pieces and put it in my allowance of water in a coconut shell. I ate each piece slowly so that it would last longer and seem to be more than it was.

The heat of the sun was so powerful that several of the men were overcome with faintness. This took away their desire to live.

We were lucky to catch two boobies in the evening. Their stomachs contained several flying fish and small cuttlefish. I saved these for dinner the next day. I was happy to see

Catching a Booby

every man thinking of this meager meal as a feast.

Wednesday, the 27th. In the evening, the clouds appeared so fixed in the West that I had little doubt we were near land. The men amused themselves talking about the things we would find.

Thursday, the 28th. At nine o'clock in the morning, we saw a great barrier of reefs we would have to pass through to get into smoother water. The sea broke away furiously over every part. I was ready to cross over the reefs no matter how dangerous it would be. But then we found a break about a mile from us, and we passed happily into the smooth water.

In these waters were the smaller islands off the mainland of New Holland (Australia). I promised to land on the first good spot we could find.

All our hardships already seemed forgotten.

A Great Barrier of Reefs

Gathering Oysters

CHAPTER 9

We Become Skin and Bones

I found a bay and a fine sandy point at which to land. Once on shore, we began to search for signs of natives. We saw some old fireplaces, but nothing that made me think that this would be an unsafe situation for the night.

Everyone was anxious to find something to eat. We soon discovered oysters on the rocks. It was nearly dark, and only a few could be gathered. I thought it best to wait till morning before deciding how to continue. Half our company slept on shore, and the other half in the boat. We would gladly have made a fire, but we could not get one started.

Friday, the 29th. There were no appearances of any of the natives being near us, so I sent some men out in search of supplies. Others were putting the boat in order so that we might be ready to go to sea hurriedly if we needed to.

The searchers returned, joyful because they had found plenty of oysters and fresh water. I had finally made a fire with the help of a small magnifying glass. More fortunate, among the few things which had been thrown into the boat and saved, we found a piece of brimstone (sulfur) and a tinderbox. The tinderbox held tinder and flint and steel. With these, I could strike a spark and start a fire easily.

One of the men had been smart enough to bring a copper pot from the ship. With a mixture of bread and a little pork, we made a

Bligh Makes a Fire.

stew that even a man who wasn't starving might have enjoyed.

Every man seemed able to bear more discomfort and weariness than I ever dreamed we would have to bear in our voyage to Timor. Despite pain, we held onto our strength.

I would not allow the men to expose themselves to the heat of the noon sun. Everyone found a piece of earth in the shade and took a short sleep.

We found some tall, flowering wire grass growing in a hollow of land—a sign that water was close. We dug there for water and soon had a well which gave us plenty of very good water.

We noticed some clear animal tracks, and Nelson agreed with me that it was the kangaroo. But we did not see any of them.

I had warned the men not to touch any kind of berry or fruit that they might find. I

A Short Sleep in the Shade

was afraid some of the fruit might be poisonous. But the men were no sooner out of my sight than they began to eat all the berries they could find. Then they became alarmed when they realized that they may have poisoned themselves. Fortunately, the fruit was wholesome and good. When I saw that this fruit was eaten by the birds, I no longer doubted its goodness.

Saturday, May the 30th. In the morning I saw that our seamen looked better, more healthy. I sent them away again to gather oysters. While they were out, I got the boat ready for sea and filled all our water vessels. We now had nearly 60 gallons. I had kept the pork under lock and key, as I did the bread. But some inconsiderate man had stolen some of it. Everyone denied knowledge of the act. To finish the matter, I portioned out the remaining pork, and after our dinner, it was gone.

The Men Eat All the Berries They Find.

We were ready for sea. We prayed for a safe journey. At four o'clock, we were preparing to embark when about twenty natives appeared, shouting and running toward us. They were naked, and their hair was bushy and short. They were each armed with a spear and a short weapon which they carried in their left hand. On the top of the hills we saw the heads of many more. They made signs for us to come to them. I thought it best to go on our way, for fear of being pursued by canoes. I passed these people as near as I dared, to get away quickly but safely.

We landed at another island at about eight o'clock in the morning. I sent two parties out to seek supplies—one to the north and the other southward. I ordered the other men to stay in the boat.

This day, weariness and weakness got the better of their sense of duty, and the men in the search parties grumbled about having to

Twenty Natives Run Toward the Launch.

work harder than their companions. They said they would rather be without dinner than go in search of it. One man went so far as to tell me, with a mutinous look, that he could be captain as well as I. I didn't know where this arguing would end if it was not stopped immediately.

I decided to keep my command or die in the attempt. I seized a cutlass and loudly ordered, "Take hold of a cutlass, man, and defend yourself!"

"You'll kill me!" he shouted out, and quickly offered his humble apologies.

I tried to cover the incident, letting it pass, and soon the whole crew was quiet again.

I walked to the highest part of the island to consider our route for the night. I located a small key, or island, which I thought would be a safer place to spend the night. As I returned to shore, I saw an old canoe, about twenty-three feet long, lying bottom up and

"Defend Yourself!"

half-buried in the beach. Its sharp bow was rudely carved in the shape of a fish head. I imagined it could carry twenty men. This discovery assured me that we needed a safer place to spend the night.

Monday, June the 1st. At dawn we reached the shore of the island. I expected that we would come upon some turtles if we stayed till night, for we saw recent tracks made by them.

As usual, I sent parties away in search of supplies. To our great disappointment, we could get only a few clams.

Towards noon, Nelson and some others who had been out returned. Nelson was so weak that he was being supported by the other two men. He was very thirsty, could not see, and could not walk. I found that he had been out too long in the hot sun without any rest. It was now that the little wine, which I had so carefully saved, became of use. I gave it to

Nelson Collapses from the Heat.

him in very small doses, with some pieces of bread in it. He soon began to recover.

I decided that we would stay the night. A quiet night's rest would be good for all those who were not well. The afternoon was also spent in sleep.

The relief which I expected from this little sleep was totally lost when one of the party let our fire spread to the grass. This rapidly made a blaze which would alert any natives to our presence. If they attacked, we had neither the arms nor strength to oppose them. After this, I anxiously waited for the flowing of the tide, so that we might put out to sea.

About midnight, the party I had sent in search of birds returned with only twelve noddies—the pigeon-sized birds we had seen earlier. Again, the folly of one of the men in the party had ruined it for us all. The man had left his two companions and disturbed

The Fire Quickly Spreads to the Grass.

the birds, so a great number of birds were lost to us.

I gave the man a good beating. He later admitted that after he separated from the other two men, he ate nine birds raw.

I tied a few shiny buttons and some pieces of iron to a tree for any of the natives who might come after us. My invalid seamen were much better for their night's rest, so we got into the launch and departed at dawn.

I divided six birds, bread, and water for dinner. I gave half a glass of wine to Nelson, who was now quite recovered.

The gunner had brought his watch with him when he left the ship. We had used it to tell time until today when it stopped. Now, the only parts of the 24 hours I can speak of accurately will be noon, sunrise, and sunset.

Wednesday, the 3rd of June. I was now fairly certain that we would begin passing New Holland in the afternoon, and we did.

A Gift is Left for the Natives.

In the evening, we once more launched into the open ocean. Miserable as our situation was, I was secretly surprised to see that no one seemed as bothered as I. Quite the opposite, the men acted as if they had started the voyage to Timor with every safety and convenience a vessel could have. I believe their confidence is one of the reasons we all survived.

I encouraged them with the hope that only eight or ten days more of travel would bring us to a land of safety. We had spent only six days along the coast of New Holland, but we had found oysters, clams, some birds, and water. This change in diet helped us. We had also been relieved of the weariness of being always in the boat, and we enjoyed good rest at night. These advantages certainly preserved our lives.

By this time, we might have sunk under our hunger or fatigue. Some would have

Launching into the Open Ocean

ceased to struggle for a life that only promised wretchedness and misery. Others, though stronger in body, would have soon followed their companions into death. Even now we were wretched objects, but the hopes of a speedy relief kept up our spirits.

Thursday, the 4th. This day we saw a number of water snakes, ringed yellow and black, and towards noon we passed a great deal of rockweed—seaweed growing on rocks. Though the weather was fair, we were constantly taking in water. This kept two men busy bailing out the boat.

Saturday, the 6th. At daylight, I found that some of the clams which had been hung up to be dried and stored were stolen. Everyone solemnly denied having any knowledge of it.

The usual ration of bread and water was served for breakfast, and the same for dinner, along with a bird which I distributed in the usual way of *Who shall have this?*

Water Snakes and Rockweed

Sunday, the 7th. The sea ran very high all this day, and we had showers of rain. We were continually wet and suffered from the night's cold. Elphinston and Lebogue, two of the hardy old seamen, appeared to be giving way very fast. I could only help them by giving them a teaspoonful or two of wine, which I had saved, expecting such an urgent need.

Monday, the 8th of June. In the afternoon we caught a small dolphin, and I gave two ounces to each man.

Tuesday, the 9th. At daylight, as usual, I heard much complaining. My own feelings told me that the men had good reason to complain. I gave Elphinston and Lebogue a little wine. After that, I could only encourage them with the hope that only a few more days would bring us to Timor.

Wednesday, the 10th. In the morning, after a very uncomfortable night, I could see that many of the men were worse. This worried

Giving the Old Seamen a Little Wine

me greatly. They were extremely weak, with swollen legs, hollow, white faces, and a constant drowsiness. I had to explain things again and again before they could think clearly enough to understand me. They looked to me like death.

Elphinston and Lebogue were the most miserable objects. I occasionally gave them a few teaspoonfuls of wine. Our hope of being able to complete our voyage was now the only real force behind our fight to stay alive.

The boatswain very innocently told me that he really thought that I looked worse than anyone in the boat. The simplicity with which he uttered such an opinion made me smile.

Thursday, the 11th. In the afternoon, we saw gannets, boobies, and many other tropical birds. We kept a very anxious lookout, and in the evening we caught a booby, which I kept for our dinner the next day.

Tropical Birds for Dinner

Friday, the 12th. In the very early morning, long before dawn, we discovered with overflowing joy the island of Timor off to the southwest. By daylight we were two leagues, or six miles, from its shore.

It is not possible for me to describe the pleasure which the sight of this land gave us. We could hardly believe that in an open boat, with so little food and water, we should have been able to reach the coast of Timor in forty-one days.

We had come 3,618 miles, and no one had perished from the hardships of the voyage. We had been attacked by savages, drenched by rains, and broiled by the sun. We had made our way through the dreadful reefs around New Holland and were now no more than skin and bones covered with rags and sores. And in all this, we lost only one man— John Norton, killed by savages on the beach.

Joyously Sighting the Island of Timor

Small Huts on Timor

CHAPTER 10

Home to England

I did not know where on Timor the Dutch settlement was, but I had a faint idea it lay at the southwest part of the island. We would have to sail around the shore to locate it. We were pleased with the general appearance of the island and saw many beautiful and cultivated spots. But we could see only a few small huts—an indication that no European lived in this part of the island.

Saturday, the 13th. In the early afternoon we came through a very dangerous breaking sea to a wide bay with an entrance about two, or three miles wide. No place could look better for shipping or more likely to be chosen for a European settlement. On a small sandy beach near the east side of the bay we saw a hut, a dog, and some cattle. We anchored the boat, and I sent the boatswain and the gunner to the hut immediately to see who lived there.

I had just time to make some notes in my journal when I saw the boatswain and the gunner returning with some of the natives. The natives said they would pilot us to the place where the governor of the island lived.

Sunday, the 14th. We continued our course around the island with the natives guiding us. We came to a channel.

The blasts of two cannons were fired from shore in welcome. This gave new life to everyone, and soon we saw two square-rigged ships and a cutter at anchor to the eastward. We had to use our oars to get in. We rowed till daylight, when we came to a small fort

The Natives Come To Help.

and a town, which the native pilot told me was Coupang, where the governor lived.

A soldier hailed us to land, and we were welcomed with great kindness. The captain of one of the vessels we had seen ordered that all my men were to be taken to his home, and he, himself, went to set up a meeting with the governor for me.

I asked my people to come on shore, which was all that some of them could do. They were hardly able to walk. With tears of joy and thanks floating down their cheeks, they were helped to the captain's house and fed tea with bread and butter. Then a surgeon dressed their sores, and the townspeople gave them clothes to wear.

When I met with the governor, he promised to provide us with food and shelter. We all stayed in the same house until we got our strength back.

When we were put off the *Bounty,* we had

Being Welcomed with Great Kindness

only enough food for five days. The mutineers must have decided that we could find shelter only at the Friendly Islands. I don't think they ever imagined we would try to return homewards. They cannot suspect that their villainy is already known of in England.

We received every kind of help, and soon showed signs of returning health. I sent descriptions of each mutineer and the *Bounty* to all the Dutch settlements, so she could be stopped if she appeared anywhere.

I purchased a 34-foot schooner, which I fitted for sea and christened the *Resource*. In her, we could reach Batavia, the capitol of Java, and join the huge fleet which sailed from there in October for Europe.

On the 20th of July, David Nelson died of a fever and was buried in the European cemetery outside of Coupang. The loss of this honest man saddened me.

By the 20th of August, we were ready for

Bligh Purchases a 34-Foot Schooner.

sea. I took an affectionate leave of the friendly people of Coupang and set sail.

On the 1st of October, we anchored in Batavia harbor. There, we found a Dutch ship of war, twenty Dutch East India ships, and many smaller vessels.

We were given food and medical care, and the seamen each received an extra month's pay in order to buy clothing for the passage to England.

We had an easy passage around the Cape of Good Hope and saw England five months later, on the 13th of March, 1790.

Of the nineteen men who were forced by the mutineers into the open launch, one was killed by savages, one died in Coupang, four died from the unhealthy weather in Java, and one died on the voyage home. But it has pleased God that twelve should overcome the difficulties and dangers of the voyage and live to arrive safely in their country.

Five Months Later—England!

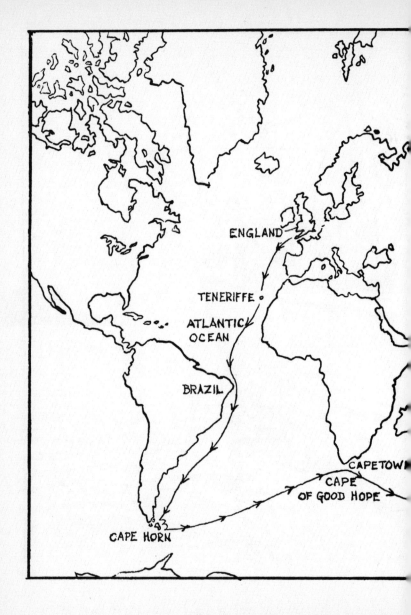

The Voyages of the *Bou*

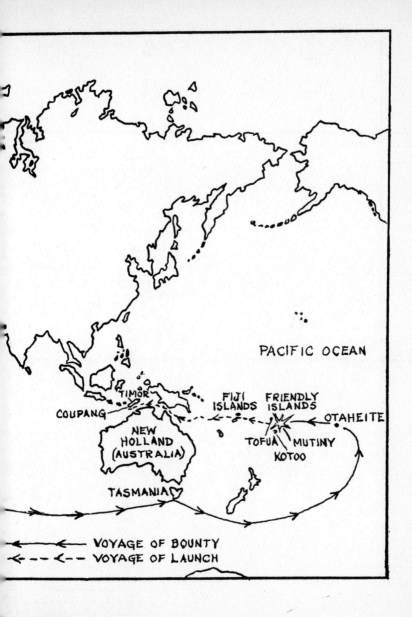

PACIFIC OCEAN

TIMOR

COUPANG

FIJI ISLANDS

FRIENDLY ISLANDS

OTAHEITE

NEW HOLLAND (AUSTRALIA)

TOFUA MUTINY

KOTOO

TASMANIA

⟵———⟵——— VOYAGE OF BOUNTY
⟵ - - ⟵ - - VOYAGE OF LAUNCH

Bligh's Launch